Growing Readers

Purchased with Smart Start Funds

Mosquitoes

by Cheryl Coughlan

Consulting Editor: Gail Saunders-Smith, Ph.D.

Consultant: Gary A. Dunn, Director of Education,
Young Entomologists' Society

Pebble Books

an imprint of Capstone Press
Mankato, Minnesota

Pebble Books are published by Capstone Press
818 North Willow Street, Mankato, Minnesota 56001
http://www.capstone-press.com

Library of Congress Cataloging-in-Publication Data
Coughlan, Cheryl.
    Mosquitoes/by Cheryl Coughlan.
    p. cm.—(Insects)
    Includes bibliographical references (p. 23) and index.
    Summary: Simple text and photographs describe the physical
characteristics of mosquitoes.
    ISBN 0-7368-0243-6
    1. Mosquitoes—Juvenile literature. [1. Mosquitoes.] I. Title. II. Series: Insects
(Mankato, Minn.)
QL536.C788   1999
595.77′2—dc21
                                                                                98-43745
                                                                                      CIP
                                                                                        AC

Note to Parents and Teachers

The Insects series supports national science standards for units on the diversity and unity of life. The series shows that animals have features that help them live in different environments. This book describes and illustrates the parts and lives of mosquitoes. The photographs support early readers in understanding the text. The repetition of words and phrases helps early readers learn new words. This book also introduces early readers to subject-specific vocabulary words, which are defined in the Words to Know section. Early readers may need assistance to read some words and to use the Table of Contents, Words to Know, Read More, Internet Sites, and Index/Word List sections of the book.

Table of Contents

Mosquitoes are insects.

6

Mosquitoes live
near water.

Mosquitoes buzz.

Mosquitoes have
a thin body.

wings

Mosquitoes have
two wings.

antennas

Mosquitoes have
two hairy antennas.

proboscis

Mosquitoes have
a proboscis.

Mosquitoes drink
plant juices.

Female mosquitoes
suck blood from
people and animals.

Words to Know

antenna—a feeler on an insect's head; mosquitoes have two hairy antennas that can sense movement.

blood—the fluid that moves through the bodies of people and animals; only female mosquitoes suck blood from people and animals.

female—an animal that can give birth to young animals or lay eggs; female mosquitoes suck blood from people and animals so their eggs can grow.

insect—a small animal with a hard outer shell, three body parts, six legs, and two antennas; insects may have two or four wings; mosquitoes have two wings and are a type of fly.

proboscis—a long, tube-shaped mouthpart; mosquitoes use their proboscis to drink plant juices and to suck blood.

wing—a movable part of an insect that helps it fly; mosquitoes beat their wings about 1,000 times each second.

Read More

Hunt, Joni Phelps. *Insects.* Closeup. Parsippany, N.J.: Silver Burdett Press, 1995.

Ryden, Hope. *ABC of Crawlers and Flyers.* New York: Clarion Books, 1996.

Snedden, Robert. *What Is an Insect?* San Francisco: Sierra Club Books for Children, 1993.

Internet Sites

Flies and Mosquitoes
http://www.ent.iastate.edu/imagegal/diptera

Mosquitoes: Pests Will Be Pests
http://www.letsfindout.com/subjects/bug/rfimosqt.html

Mosquito Alert
http://whyfiles.news.wisc.edu/016skeeter/index.html

Index/Word List

Word Count: 39
Early-Intervention Level: 7

Editorial Credits

Damian C. Koshnick, editor; Timothy Halldin, cover designer; Kimberly Danger,
    photo researcher

Photo Credits

Bill Johnson, 10, 12, 18, 20
David M. Dennis/Tom Stack and Associates, 14
Dwight R. Kuhn, cover, 4, 6, 8, 16
GeoIMAGERY/Joe Warfel, 1